Visit www.CristinApril.com for free c

A very special thank you goes out to
Rachel Gillham, who colored the badass cover!

Colored pages on the back cover by: (left to right)

Shawn Hallenback | Shelly Pfeiffer | Megan Page | Michelle Huntley-Herrema | Jennifer Scarabin | Jennifer Scarabin

Jennifer Scarabin | Kim Fulmer | Jennifer Scarabin | Jennifer Scarabin | Lina Weikel | Kelly Taylor

Tracy Lasseter | Kelly Taylor | Dawn Meredith | Lina Weikel | Kim Fulmer | Gayla Albert

Domineek Bumpas | Jennifer Scarabin | Kelly Taylor | John Taylor | Lisa Frey | Lina Weikel

Jessica Johnson | Lina Weikel | Molly Wee | Lina Weikel | Shawn Hallenbeck | Tracy Lasseter

The only thing more fun than making a sassy coloring book is to see the pages of the book colored by others! Please share them with me!

#cristinaprilsart

Facebook: www.facebook.com/cristinaprilsart
Twitter: www.twitter.com/cristinapril
Instagram: www.instagram.com/cristinapril
Pinterest: www.pinterest.com/cristinapril

About the Artist: Cristin April is a self-taught artist who loves doodling, lettering, and sarcasm. She has combined these into hand-drawn, original coloring pages for others to enjoy. Cristin resides in upstate New York with her rescue dogs, her rescue husband, her daughter, and lots of coffee and wine.

If you enjoy this book, please leave a review on Amazon.com!

This book is dedicated to my Mom who was a feisty badass woman, always spoke her mind, and was my biggest supporter. Miss you, Mom!

Much love and thanks to my coloring team, "The Sassy Squad" who help promote my work. You can read their bios and learn more about them at CristinApril.com.

Check out my page at www.patreon.com/CristinApril to support my work and get exclusive monthly rewards.

Many thanks to my sassy, badass Patreon supporters:

Scott Frey	Jennifer Scarabin
Kim Fulmer	Lina Weikel
Robin Nelson	Michelle Turner
Jennifer Stahl	Kathryn Beyers
Susan Nicita	Jen Kohnen
Ruth Henke	Hollie Cameron
Linda Adams	Jessica Johnson

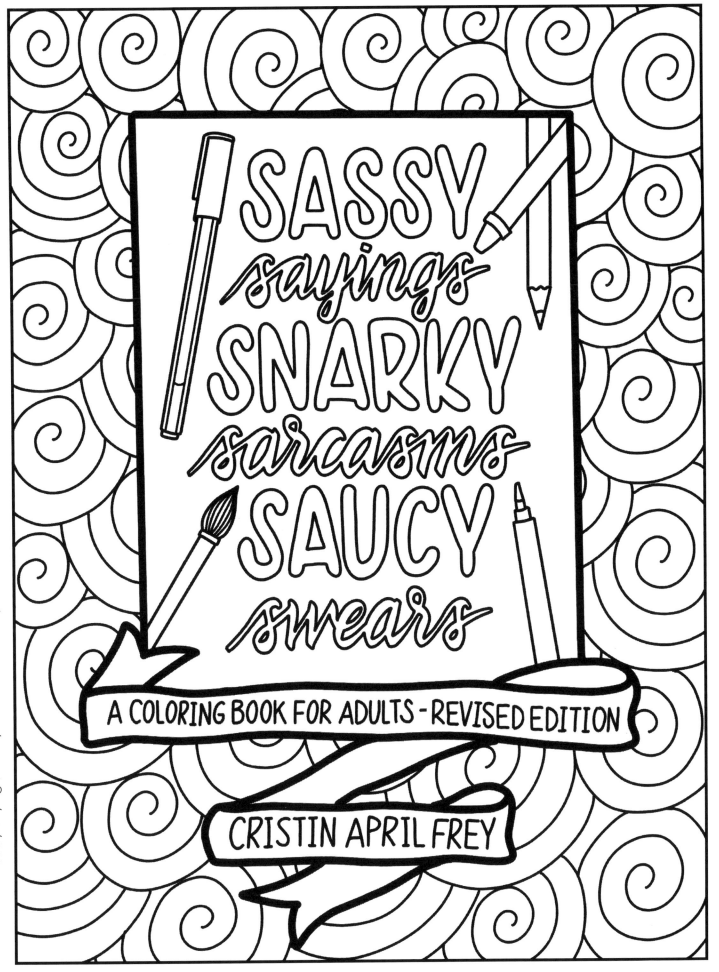

I'm not a *princess*... I don't need saving.

I'm a *queen*... I got this shit handled.

IF I EVER LET MY HEAD DOWN IT WILL BE JUST TO ADMIRE MY SHOES.
—MARILYN MONROE—

Oh, for sake!

IF I WERE A BIRD
I KNOW WHO I'D SHIT ON

KISS MY SASS

CRISTINAPRIL.COM

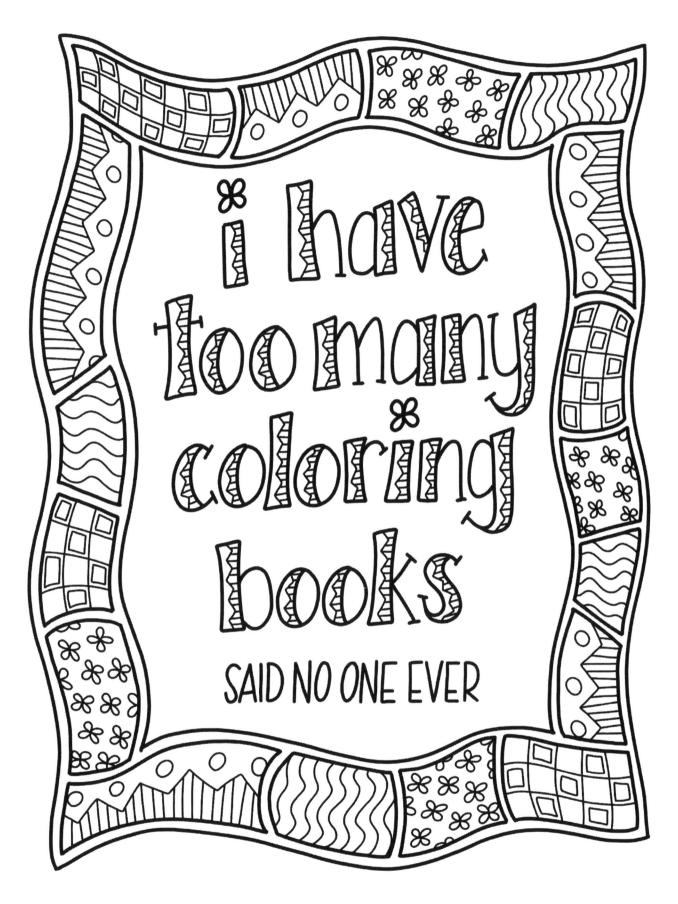

i have too many coloring books

SAID NO ONE EVER

COLOR TESTING PAGE

CRISTINAPRIL.COM

fuck FUCK FUCK fuck
FUCK fuck FUCK fuck
FUCK fuck FUCK fuck
#$!✳% FUCK fuck FUCK
fuck fuck FUCK fuck
fuck fuck FUCK FUCK
FUCK FUCK fuck FUCK
fuck FUCK FUCK fuck
FUCK FUCK fuck FUCK
fuck FUCK fuck FUCK
FUCK FUCK FUCK FUCK
FUCK fuck FUCK fuck

Today's Recipe:
2 cups cluster
1 cup fuck

SAMPLE PAGE

from "The Art of Not Giving a Fuck: A Callous
Adult Coloring Book of Disregard"
by Cristin April Frey

THE ART OF
NOT
GIVING
A FUCK

A CALLOUS ADULT COLORING BOOK OF DISREGARD

CRISTIN APRIL FREY

THE CHAINS ON MY MOOD SWING JUST SNAPPED

MENOPAUSAL MANIA & MAYHEM

AN ADULT COLORING BOOK OF HORMONAL HERESY

CRISTIN APRIL FREY

SAMPLE PAGE

from "50 Nifty Coloring Pages:
An On-the-Go Adult Coloring Book"
by Cristin April Frey

52000203R00046